ONTENTS

D1313911

MATERIALS NEEDED

- Ruler
- Glass Cleaner
- Scissors
- Cotton Swabs
- Steel Wool
- Masking Tape
- Carbon Paper (smudge proof)
- Contact Adhesive Shelving Vinyl
- Additional Patterns & Designs
- Newspaper or Plastic Drop Cloth
- Protective Glasses or Goggles
- Pen, Pencil, and Eraser
- Long Sleeve Garment & Apron
- Paper Towels

tching glass is a re-discovered technique for leisure-time activity, with which glass can be attractively decorated and personalized with drawings, ornaments, and calligraphy.

A nicely etched glass looks beautiful as well as decorative and valuable. Etched glasses look the best when displayed against a dark background and illuminated from the side.

Glass Etching as a craft has many advantages. It is suitable for most age groups, only a few tools are required, and acceptable glass items can be purchased locally with an assortment of shapes, sizes, and colors available.

You can etch glass at home as a hobby or as a business, or you can gather together family and friends for an afternoon of glass decorating. No special talent or drawing ability is required. The beginner or experienced glass etcher can select from a wide variety of patterns. Each completed project brings satisfaction, and reveals your personal touch. With increasing experience you will use larger, more demanding patterns and will soon be creating patterns of your own.

There is hardly a more beautiful or personal gift than a glass etched with someone's initials or a few words to celebrate that special day or occasion!

How to Create Your Own Custom Glass Etching Stencil

This section of our Glass Etching Guide will teach you the easiest method we have found to enable you to reproduce almost any idea, pattern or artwork into a finished etched design. We strongly recommend using Contact A-21 adhesive-backed vinyl shelf covering for most custom stencil projects! This product offers consistent quality, inexpensive cost and superior adhesive strength when applied to glass.

Step one: Clean the glass or mirror.

Clean the glass or mirror thoroughly to remove all grease, dust, and finger prints. Use our glass cleaner concentrate or a commercial window or glass cleaner. Dry the glass or mirror thoroughly.

Step two: Cutting the adhesive-backed vinyl

Cut the vinyl masking about an inch or two larger than the width and length of the glass or mirror project. Do not remove the protective backing yet.

Save all your cut off scraps of vinyl because they can used for smaller projects or for filling areas on larger glass and mirror projects.

Step three: Applying the vinyl masking

Turn the vinyl masking over with the

Some helpful hints before we get started.

A. Rubbing the masking vinyl with steel wool before you trace your design, will give you a darker impression to work with.

B. The longer the vinyl masking remains on the glass, the better the adhesive sticks.

C. For a better bond, place a paper towel over the vinyl masking and use a warm iron to lightly press against the towel to help activate the adhesive

D. We recommend that you start with a simple design for your first glass etching project and gradually work up to more intricate patterns once you gain confidence and experience with the knife cutting techniques. Now let's get started!

7

backing sheet facing up as shown in photo A1. Peel down about 2" of the backing sheet across the top of the vinyl. Press down and crease the

backing sheet to force it to lay flat. Turn the vinyl sheet over. Using the sides and bottom edge of the masking vinyl, position the vinyl on the glass, allowing it to overlap the glass evenly all around. When aligned, press the area you folded back to adhere the vinyl to the glass. With one hand on top of the vinyl, rub from side to side to adhere it

to the glass. With your other hand underneath, slowly pull to remove the backing sheet.

Press out the air bubbles as you go. If you miss a few, pull up the vinyl masking until the bubbles disappear, then continue rubbing from side to side until the vinyl is evenly applied. Fold the excess vinyl over the edges of the glass. See photo A2.

Step four: Transferring your design onto the vinyl masking

There are four techniques we use to transfer designs before they are cut by hand to create a glass etching stencil.

1. **Trace your design.** Position your design in the desired location on the vinyl covered glass. Use a ruler to determine if your design is aligned on all sides. Tape only the top edge of the design sheet firmly to the masking vinyl. See photo

A3. The design is taped only on the top edge so it may be lifted periodically to check how the design is transferring. Place

a sheet of smudge proof carbon paper face down under the design sheet and trace over the design with a ball point pen. Use enough pressure to transfer the design but not so hard that you tear the design sheet. Upon completion of the tracing, lift up the design sheet and carbon paper to make sure all lines were transferred accurately. If so, then remove both sheets.

2. **Draw your design freehand.** If you have artistic ability you can try your hand using a rounded pencil and light pressure to avoid tearing the vinyl.

3. **Create a stencil from cardboard.** Use a cardboard stencil to help guide your pencil. Good for repeat patterns.

4. **Use a photocopy of your design.** Use a copy machine to duplicate your design. Then coat the back of the photocopy with spray adhesive and rub the design to glue it to the vinyl.

> **Helpful Hint:**
> We have found that when you etch large open areas of a design, the natural textures and striations of the glass (which are invisible to the eye) sometimes show up after etching. To avoid this problem, pick designs with more detailed areas or add more detail to large open areas of existing designs.

Illustration 1

Illustration 2

Illustration 3

Step five: Select the areas to be etched

Every design has several possibilities of how it can be cut out as a stencil and etched. You can choose to cut only the outline of the design or you may choose to cut only the solid areas or you may combine both techniques. See illustrations.

If you are unsure as to which technique to use, take your original design sheet and use a pencil to shade in the areas you think would look good as an etched area or outlined area.

Step six: Cutting out the design.

It is a good idea to practice on a scrap piece of glass before you start your first project. When you see the design after it is cut out, you will be able to judge the finished results and will be able to make any changes and edit the design if needed. Practice also gives you the chance to get acquainted with the feel of the hobby knife and develop better control of the blade. We recommend that you purchase a standard hobby knife with replaceable blades like an Xacto Knife or similar type. Make sure your blade is sharp before you begin. A dull blade will tear the vinyl instead of cutting it with unsatisfactory results.

going to be etched in a later section of this guide. See photo A4.

If for some reason you are not happy with the stencil you have finished, or the design just wasn't right, you can remove the remaining masking, start over again from step one. You are not committed to the design until the etch cream is applied.

Step seven: Prepare for etching

Use a lint-free cloth wrapped around your finger to press down firmly on all the cut edges of the stencil to avoid any lifting areas. Lightly clean all exposed areas with a clean cloth that is slightly dampened (not wet) with window cleaner.

Pat dry being very careful not to disturb the vinyl

Hold the hobby knife in your hand as you would a pen for writing. Rest the weight of your hand on the side of your palm and grip the knife handle firmly but not too tight.

Slowly and smoothly pull the knife along the side of the line using just enough pressure to cut through the vinyl. Guide the blade along the design turning the glass when needed to insure proper hand position to avoid hand fatigue and discomfort.

When using the Outline Technique, you must cut on both sides of the line (parallel cuts) and remove the vinyl from the center area. When you are using the Solid Area Technique you only need to cut on the outside of the design line then remove the vinyl.

It is important that your cut lines connect the start and finish of each area and you avoid cutting past the point where lines meet.

After all the lines have been cut, use the tip of your knife blade to pry under the cut edges

Photo A4

and carefully lift up the pieces of vinyl. Grip them with your fingers and slowly peel up making sure all the lines have been cut re-cut if needed.

Proceed to pull off all the cut vinyl areas where your design is to etched. Wherever the glass is exposed, it is

CHECK LIST

☑ *Work area, etching cream, and project temperature must be over 65 degrees*

☑ *Good ventilation needed in work area*

☑ *Cover work table with newspaper*

☑ *Work near running water source*

☑ *Wear long sleeved garment*

☑ *Wear protective glasses or goggles*

☑ *Wear rubber or plastic gloves*

☑ *Have your brush nearby*

Hand-cut geometrical shapes create a primitive look to this contemporary vase.

Glass Etching Cream in order for the chemical to react properly on the glass or mirror. You should not be able to see your design through the etch cream. Work quickly and safely.

Dip the brush into the etch cream and apply a very thick layer covering the entire design. See photo A5.

Although Armour Etch reacts instantly upon contact with the glass, when using Contact A21 masking vinyl as a stencil, allow the etching cream to remain on the glass for up to five minutes. Etching times vary with the type of stencil used.

Larger projects require the use of a larger soft bristle brush. When etching larger projects, it is actually easier to pour the etch cream directly onto the glass while working quickly to cover entire design.

Armour Etch Cream has a shelf life of over 3 years if kept tightly closed. It can be extended by placing the closed jar in very hot water for 15-30 minutes. This process blends the crystals in the cream reactivating it producing a smooth consistency.

While you wait for the etching cream to react, use your brush to gently move the cream to

Photo A5

masking. If you are cleaning very small areas, use a Q-Tip. double check the exposed glass to be sure all finger prints and vinyl residue have been removed from these surfaces.

Step eight: Applying Armour Etch® Glass Etching Cream

You must apply a thick layer of Armour Etch

Helpful Hint:
When working on motor vehicles and other vertical glass surfaces, tape a plastic drop cloth on the bottom and partially up the sides of the design to protect the paint and direct the rinse water into a bucket.

make sure there are no air bubbles or missed areas. Armour Etch actually dissolves away a layer of glass and permanently frosts the remaining glass.

Important: *Porcelain and Enamel sinks will lose their shine after repeatedly being subjected to rinses of diluted Armour Etch Cream.*

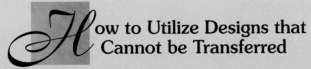

How to Utilize Designs that Cannot be Transferred

When you come across a pattern you want to etch, but you are unable to utilize the original source for a tracing guide (For example: library books, album covers, wallpaper on the wall, etc.) trace the pattern onto tracing paper or photocopy. Then use the copy with a carbon underneath.

How to enlarge or reduce a pattern

Enlarge:

The simplest method for enlarging a pattern is to draw squares on the original design. The squares must all be a uniform size. (See diagram 1) Then draw larger squares to enlarge the pattern. Example: If you want the design 4 times larger than the original, the large set of squares must be 4 times the size of the original squares. (See diagram 2) The number of large squares must equal the number of small squares.

Number the squares of the small and large squares consecutively. First in the horizontal direction across the top and then in a vertical direction down the left side of the pattern. (See the diagrams) Slowly copy the design square by square. Use the numbers of the squares as a guide. Check the proportion of your copied pattern in each square to maintain the original design.

Reduce:

Use the same method mentioned above, but in reverse. Draw smaller squares and transfer your pattern square by square.

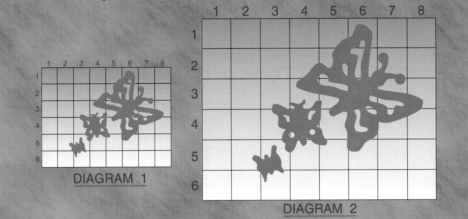

DIAGRAM 1

DIAGRAM 2

Opaque Projectors:

There are opaque projectors available, some at reasonable prices, for the purpose of enlarging or reducing designs. They are found in art supply stores, electronic equipment supply stores, photography stores and some hobby & craft stores. This is a worth while investment for people who are planning on going into business for themselves producing custom etched designs.

With the assistance of an opaque projector you can combine several parts of designs to create a new designs.

Professional enlarged or reduced artwork:

Check to see if there is an establishment in your area which will enlarge or reduce a pattern for you. Check photography stores and outlets. Your neighborhood hobby & craft store might be able to advise you where you can find such a place.

Step Nine: Rinse off Armour Etch® Glass Etching Cream

When rinsing off the etching cream, use a low to medium water pressure to prevent ripping, tearing, or removing any of the vinyl stencil material. Rinse from the top of the project down, work quickly and use your brush to help. See photo A6.

Use plenty of water and wash thoroughly until all etching cream residue is removed. Avoid splashing! The etched effect will not show up until the glass is rinsed and completely dried.

Once the rinsing and drying is done you can start removing the vinyl masking. Most larger pieces will come off pretty easy. If you have trouble with all those smaller pieces, use window cleaner, a plastic dish scrubber.

We would like to repeat that it is not recommended that you attempt to etch large solid areas of glass or mirror or attempt to create reverse etched designs where the design is clear and the background is completely etched. The reason for this recommendation is that because you are applying the etching cream by hand there is the possibility that the finished etched area will show a uneven, blotchy effect. Also glass can have invisible stains and marks that show up when etched.

Photo A6

A Timeless Art—Etched In Glass

Since its creation some 3500 years ago, artists have sought ways to enhance the shimmering appearance of glass. Lovers of art and beauty, as far back as the ancient Egyptians, have been decorating with it and on ti for centuries. First, craftsmen added color. Then, they ground into it with copper wheels and carved it with diamond bits to leave beautiful and intricate engravings.

Perhaps the most secretive method of altering the surface was that of glass etching. It was a carefully protected craft because of the dangerous chemical process used to produce the milky, frosted finish. Craftsmen used hydrofluoric acid to etch delicate patterns and pictures over the surfaces of windows, mirrors, lanterns, glass gloves, vases, and more.

First, beeswax was spread over the glass to mask the areas that were to remain clear. Then, craftsmen carefully cut a negative image of their pattern into the beeswax. The acid would settle into the pattern and form everything from landscapes to portraits, figures, and animals.

About 100 years ago, the chemical formulation used in modern glass etching was invented, improving the whole process and making it safer for industrial use. This formula may have been responsible for the rebirth of etching in Victorian homes. Etched glass adorned windows in the grand entryways of many lovely turn-of-the-century homes. It enhanced the beauty of the window without obscuring daylight as stained glass windows did.

The process was made even safer and easier 25 years ago with the introduction of etching cream.

Paired with modern plastic stencils, this easy-to-use method has inspired many at-home crafters to take up the art. Precut stencils in a variety of sizes and patterns make it easy to emulate favorite designs and motifs.

Now even dabblers in the art can enjoy the finished effects of etching on virtually any plain or colored glass surface, from decorative boxes and goblets, to windows, mirrors, and more!

Rub 'N' Etch® Pre-cut, Rub-on Stencils

*T*his section of our Glass Etching Guide will teach you how to use our exclusive Rub'N'Etch Stencils. With this method you'll be creating small, delicate etching your very first try in just a few minutes time!

Step one: Clean the glass or mirror

Clean the glass or mirror in order to remove all grease, dust, and any finger prints. Use our Super Cleaner or a commercial type window or glass cleaner. to dry the glass or mirror thoroughly.

Step two: Select design and cut from sheet

Select the stencil for your project and carefully cut the stencil from the larger sheet. It is important to keep both the blue stencil sheet and the frosted backing sheet together to avoid touching the back side of the stencil sheet.

Step three: Measure and tape stencil in position

Measure carefully to determine where you will locate the stencil on the glass or mirror. Separate the blue stencil sheet from the frosted backing sheet. Place the blue stencil on the glass with the blue (slightly tacky) side touching the glass. Secure the stencil temporarily in place with four pieces of masking tape to keep the stencil from moving while applying it to the glass.

Step four: Apply stencil to glass

Using a wood burnisher stick, begin to rub the stencil sheet to transfer the actual stencil to the glass surface. Rub firmly with smooth even

Photo B1

strokes but do not dig into the stencil. It helps to hold the wood stick at a higher angle. As the stencil transfers to the surface of the glass, it will change color from dark blue to a light blue. Be sure to rub over all areas including fine lines even areas under the masking tape. See photo B1.

Step five: Removing top carrier sheet

When the entire stencil has been adhered, carefully take off some of the masking tape and slowly peel back, but do not completely remove, the top sheet exposing the blue stencil that's adhered to the glass. Photo B2.

If the stencil has not been completely adhered to the glass, carefully retape the top sheet in place and re-rub this area until all the pieces have been adhered. When finished, remove top carrier sheet.

Step six: Preparing and protecting the glass for the etching process

Apply a border of household masking tape around the entire stencil overlapping the tape on the blue stencil material by 1/16" to 1/8". This overlap is very important because it prevents the etching cream from seeping onto the glass and etching unwanted areas! Now use the frosted white backing sheet you removed in step 3 and lightly rub over the entire stencil and masking tape to insure

Photo B2

17

all the tape edges and stencil pieces are laying flat on the glass. See photo B3. Check the stencil for small tears or pin holes by holding the

glass up to a light. If any holes appear, use pieces of masking tape to cover them but be careful, the tape can tear the stencil if you try to move apiece of tape already adhered to the stencil.

Step seven: Applying the Armour Etch Glass Etching Cream

For best etching results we recommend that the room temperature, etching cream, and project you are etching on be over 65

degrees. Cover your work area with newspaper, work in a well lit, well ventilated room near a water source. Wear protective goggles and plastic gloves. You must apply a thick layer of etching cream in order for the chemical to react properly on the glass

project. You should not be able to see the design through this layer of etch cream. Dab on the etching cream and stay within the taped area. See photo B4.

Step eight: Washing off the etching cream

The Armour Etch® Glass Etching Cream must remain on the glass for only one Minute Maximum

No longer! Then immediately wash off all traces of etching cream under cool to warm water. See photo B5. If you allow the etching cream to remain on the Rub'N'Etch Stencil for more than one minute, there is a possibility that the finished etched design will have "fuzzy" edges which is undesirable! You may use your brush to help speed up the removal of the etching cream. You want to work as quickly and safely as pos-

Photo B5

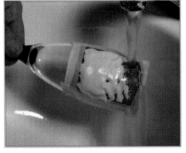

sible at this point. It is O.K. if some pieces of blue stencil come off too. Do Not let the rinse water touch any of the exposed glass because it contains diluted etching cream and might cause permanent etched stains and ruin your project! It is always better to mask off to protect everything then have a problem at the end.

Complimentary or coordinating stencils often can be used to accentuate an already attractive glass piece as with this star bottle with moon & star etching.

Step nine: Remove stencil and masking tape

After washing off all the etching cream, peel back and remove masking tape along with the remaining blue stencil pieces. See photo B6.

Stubborn stencil pieces can be removed by using some window cleaner and paper towel. Clean your project thoroughly. There you have it! Custom glass etching at far

Photo B6

below the custom price, and best of all you did it yourself. Be prepared for a lot of "Who did it?" and "How much?" from your family, friends, and customers!

Calligraphy Styled Lettering System

This unique lettering system makes it easier for everyone to create custom names, dates, and messages to decorate glassware for gift giving and special occasions. Perfect for wedding glasses, anniversary presents, birthdays, business gifts and more...

Step One: Calligraphy Lettering Placement

There are a few different techniques that can be used to align the calligraphy lettering. The shape of the project and whether it is glass or mirror will determine which one of following techniques you will use........

A. Draw a line onto a piece of paper. Tape the piece of paper behind the clear glass facing up towards you. This works best with a flat piece of clear glass.

B. Take a piece of masking tape and place the tape in position slightly below where the bottom of the lettering will be placed.

You can measure with a ruler in several spots to be sure that the tape is evenly placed horizontally. Masking tape can easily be re-positioned if you need to correct the alignment.

C. Draw a line with a fine line grease pencil.

Step two: Applying the Calligraphy Lettering stencil to the glass

Cut the stencil sheet into strips to make it easier to align and rub down the letters, Photo D1.

Once you have established a flat line for alignment, you can start to rub down the letters (see photo D2). Use the bottom edge of the little blue square that contains your letter and place that bottom edge onto the alignment line. In most cases you can start with the UPPER CASE letter first, followed by the lower case lettering.

Each letter should slightly overlap the previous letter. If you are going to be writing a lot of copy, it is a good idea to first write your message onto a piece of paper, then copy letter for letter onto the glass.

If you are going to center your copy, look at your copy on paper and find the center letter. Count the first upper case letter as (2) two or (3) three if it is very wide (ie "W"). Place your center letter in the center of your work area and work out to the left and then to the right, overlapping each letter or number slightly each time you add another letter.

Step three: Protecting the areas of your project

Once all the lettering is in place, the next step is to tape all around the outer edges of your completed words or names, overlapping some of the blue edges of the stencil with masking tape to prevent the etching cream from seaping onto the glass. Be careful NOT to COVER any of the open letter areas with the tape. In some cases you might have to cut the masking tape narrower to fit into tight spaces. See photo D3.

Step four: Applying the Armour Etch Glass Etching Cream

Apply a thick layer of Armour Etch Glass Etching Cream in order for the chemical to react properly on the glass or mirror. You should not be able to see your design through the etch cream. Work quickly and safely.

Dip the brush into the etch cream and apply a very thick layer covering the entire design. The Armour Etch Glass Etching Cream must remain on the glass for only one Minute Maximum No longer! Then immediately wash off all traces of etching cream under cool to warm water.

Special Effects

Create the look of old sterling silver by enhancing your finished etched project with an application of a semi-permanent wax. It is best to use this special effect for display pieces that will not require repeated washings. Washing, especially in the dishwasher, will remove the brilliance of the wax, and eventually, the entire layer.

1. Above is a photo of a finished etched glass with a Kokopelli Indian design.

2. Use a cotton swab to apply a thick layer of the metallic wax onto the area that has been etched.

3. Immediately take a paper towel and wipe off the excess metallic wax. The wax will only adhere to the etched design. A second application can be applied, if needed.

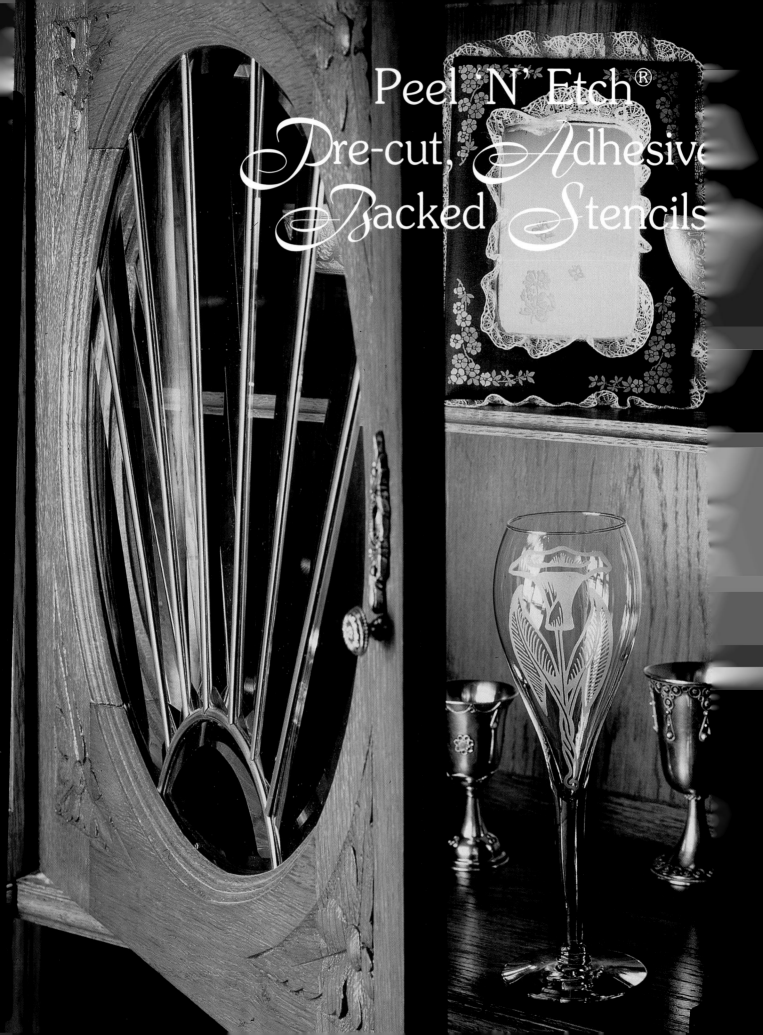

Peel 'N' Etch®
Pre-cut, Adhesive
Backed Stencils

*T*his section of our Glass Etching Guide will teach you how to use our larger PEEL'N'ETCH® Stencils. They are adhesive-backed, range in size from 4" x 4" up to 24" x 30" and can also be sandblasted.

PEEL'N'ETCH is a pre-cut vinyl stencil that is sandwiched between a top carrier sheet and a waxed backing sheet. These stencils can be used on most non-porous surfaces. For example: Glass, Mirror, Plastic, Metal, and Finished Woods.

Step one: Clean the glass or mirror

Clean the glass or mirror in order to remove grease, dust, and all finger prints. Dry the glass or mirror thoroughly. See Photo C1.

Photo C1

Step two: Measure to determine proper location

Carefully measure the stencil design as well as the glass or mirror with a ruler to determine where you will locate the stencil on your project. Do not assume the stencil design is centered on the stencil vinyl. Mark location using a marker.

Step three: Remove waxed backing sheet

Turn the stencil over so the waxed backing sheet is facing up. Slowly peel off the entire backing sheet by pulling the sheet back onto itself at approximately 180 degree angle. See photo C2. If any stencil pieces stick to the backing sheet, Stop pulling and press the backing sheet over the pieces onto the stencil until the piece re-adheres itself to the stencil.

Photo C2

Step four: Applying the stencil

Hold the stencil in your hands and turn it over so the exposed adhesive side is now facing down. Bend up the two sides of the stencil so that the center is bowed down. Use your measurement marks to align the stencil as you bring it closer to the glass before actually touching it to the glass surface. When you apply the stencil to your project, make sure the bowed center part of the stencil touches first. Once the center

touches the surface, use the palm of your hand to smooth out the stencil to the left and then to the right. See photo C3.

Photo C3

Step five: Removing the top carrier sheet

After the stencil has been completely adhered, carefully peel back the top carrier sheet to remove it. As with the backing sheet, pull the top sheet back on to itself at a 180 degree angle to avoid pulling up pieces of the stencil. If some stencil pieces do pull up, simply use the top sheet to press down these areas until the are re-adhered to the surface.

Step six: Peeling out the design

On the opposite side of the PEEL'N'ETCH instructions is a black and white diagram of the stencil design. Using this diagram as a guide, remove all the small stencil sections shown in white. Use the point of your hobby knife, tweezer, or a pin to remove the stencil pieces. Take your time, pay close attention to what you are doing! See photo C4. After you remove all the stencil pieces from areas to be etched, place the

waxed backing sheet over the top of the stencil. With the palm of your of your hand, a roller, burnisher, or credit card, press firmly in a back & forth, up & down motion to adhere the stencil to the surface of your project.

Use masking tape or Contact A-21 vinyl to completely cover and protect all the surrounding exposed areas of glass. Make sure you overlap the vinyl or tape onto the stencil material to prevent the etching cream from seeping underneath.

Step seven: Apply etching cream

Be sure that all exposed glass or mirror is completely clean. All edges of the remaining stencil must lie flat against the glass surface. All exposed glass other than design area, must also be covered with Contact Vinyl or tape. The glass, room temperature, and the Armour Etch Cream must be over 65 degrees. Apply a thick layer of etching cream with

a soft bristle brush. The etching cream should be applied thick enough so the design is not visible. Allow the etching cream to remain on the glass about 5 to 6 minutes. While waiting, use your brush to re-distribute the etching cream by re-brushing the cream in different directions to insure proper coverage and eliminate air pockets. See photo C5

Step eight: Wash off etching cream

Using a medium pressure water source, wash off all the remaining etching cream working from top to bottom. Work quickly but safely! Avoid splashing, wear eye protection and gloves.

Step nine: Remove stencil

Once the rinsing and drying is done you can start removing the vinyl masking. Most larger pieces will come off pretty easy. If you have trouble with all those smaller pieces, use window cleaner, a plastic dish scrubber.

We would like to repeat that it is not recommended that you attempt to etch large solid areas of glass or mirror or attempt to create reverse etched designs where the design is clear and the background is completely etched. The reason for this recommendation is that because you are applying the etching cream by hand there is the possibility that the finished etched area will show a uneven, blotchy effect.

Also glass can have invisible stains and marks that show up when etched.

When you etch the glass by sandblasting you are actually creating rough, obscure areas to contrast with the smooth, clear areas of the glass. This is accomplished by mixing abrasive grit with air under pressure and directing the stream at the areas of the glass you wish to etch. The abrasive will remove tiny pieces of glass from the surface resulting in an etched, frosted finish.

Abrasives

The most common types of abrasives used for glass etching are aluminum oxide and silicone carbide. Although these abrasives are more expensive than silica sand, they are actually more economical to use than regular silica sand because they can be recycled many times and save labor because they cut into the glass much faster. Aluminum oxide is a widely used abrasive for etching glass but it generates static electricity which causes the dust to stick to the back of the glass making it difficult to see what your blasting. Silicone

Blasting Direction

Resist Material | Resist Material
Glass | Glass

Blasting Direction

Resist Material | Resist Material
Glass | Glass

carbide is considered the cadillac of abrasives because it is the fastest cutting and the longest lasting of all the abrasives. Instead of dulling as it is used, silicone carbide breaks into smaller particles creating new sharp, cutting edges. But, it too will eventually break down to dust which will be too fine to blast with.

Abrasives are referred to by size or grit number..the smaller the particles the higher the grit number. Larger grit will cut faster, leave a coarser finish, and generate more heat. The smaller grit size will cut slower and leave a finer, smoother finish. The most common grit sizes for etching windows and architectural size projects are 100 to 150 grit. For a finer finish on glassware and trophies 150 to 200 grit is used. For small micro blasters or pen type blasters use 220 to 400 grit. When blasting wood signs we recommend grit sizes of 30 to 80.

Resists

When you decide to etch a design on your glass or mirror project, you must determine which parts of the glass will be etched and which parts will be clear. You accomplish this by covering the glass with a vinyl or rubber material called a resist. because it resists the abrasive and prevents the etching of certain parts of the glass. Your design is drawn onto the resist or you can use a photocopy glued to the resist...You then

Important: Silica sand contains free silica which is considered a hazardous material. Aluminum oxide and silicone carbide are considered nuisance dusts and are therefore safer to use.

begin hand cutting the design using an exacto type hobby knife. When all the areas of the design have been cut, you remove areas of the resist where you want the etching to be created.

Resist is specified by its thickness, usually stated in mils, and by the type of material, typically vinyl or rubber. Selecting the proper resist for the job is very important. Controlling cost is essential for making a profit. You want to use the least expensive resist that is adequate for the job. You don't want to use a resist that is too thin and might blow off under pressure, and you certainly don't want to use an expensive, rubber resist that is heavier than needed. Heavier resists are thicker and more difficult to cut and blast finer details.

For most shading and surface etching a 4 mil vinyl is recommended. For shading and light carving 4-8 mil vinyl is appropriate. Medium depth carving demands a 10-15 mil vinyl but it is thick, hard, and difficult to cut. When it comes to medium to deep carving of glass you should be using a rubber resist, usually

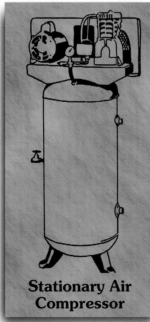

Stationary Air Compressor

between 18 and 30 mil. We also use the 4 mil vinyl, inexpensive 5 mil polyethylene, or even contact shelving vinyl to protect the back of the project as well as any areas that need to remain unetched. You can easily over-spray or scratch the glass when working with abrasives. A little bit of preventive preparation goes a long way.

Pre-cut Stencils

Hand cutting can be tedious and time consuming so whenever you can, use a pre-cut stencil..

There are a large assortment of adhesive backed 4 mil stencils available that can save you lots of time and energy when creating etched projects.

Portable Air Compressor

Choosing The Right Air Compressor

The air compressor is the machine that creates the compressed air needed to run the sandblaster. We have found that the smallest compressor you can use to power your sandblaster is a two horsepower unit that generates at least 6 CFM at 100 PSI. CFM represents the cubic feet of air per minute or amount of air the compressor generates and PSI means pressure per square inch or air pressure the compressor puts out.A siphon blaster requires more cfm per 100 psi to work efficiently, while a pressure blaster requires less cfm. Even though pressure systems are more expensive than siphon systems the increased speed at which they etch the glass more than compensates for the added expense. Make sure the compressor you choose has an air tank of at least 20 gallons. The larger the air tank the less the compressor has to run to fill the air tank to the proper air pressure. Check the specifications of the sandblaster you are purchasing to determining the size of the compressor you will need. Your budget and the type of blaster will be the final factor in choosing the right compressor.

Cutting Tools

There are many types of knives available to make the process of handcutting your design easier. The xacto or hobby knife is the most common knife used but there are swivel knives, dual blade cutting knives and you can even use a bow compass with a cutting blade to cut circles. It is

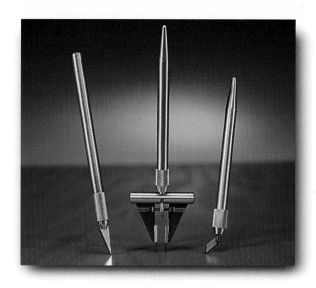

also beneficial to purchase a metal ruler to make cutting straight lines more accurate.

Sandblasters

Siphon System

This is the least expensive system, but it requires a larger compressor to function correctly. This particular system uses a siphon or suction to pull the abrasive from the container through the hose and out the nozzle of the gun. The air pressure required for a siphon system is 80-100 PSI.

Pressure System

A pressure sandblaster is a bit more sophisticated and more expensive than the siphon system. This type of blaster uses much less air from the compressor and etches the glass more rapidly because the abrasive is placed in a container that is pressurized and this feeds the abrasive more efficiently into the air stream and out the nozzle. Most pressure blasters operate at 40 PSI and etch 3 to 4 times faster than a siphon blaster operating at 100 PSI.

Sandblasting Cabinet

For convenience and ease of glass etching, nothing beats the blasting cabinet. It is safer to use and actually makes glass etching much more enjoyable. Most blasting cabinets come with a siphon blasting system built in, the abrasive is siphoned from the hopper in the bottom of the cabinet.

An interior light illuminates the work area, allowing you to see more clearly and with less fatigue. The only disadvantage with a blasting cabinet is that you are limited by the size of the cabinet when determining how large the glass or mirror project can be.

Siphon Blaster

Pressure Blaster

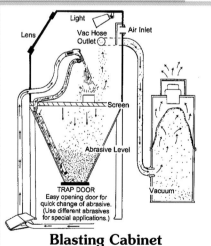

Blasting Cabinet

Strip Silver Mirror Removing System

We included this section on mirror removing because it is the perfect compliment to creative glass etching.

The Strip Silver system enables you to strip out clear windows within the mirrored area. You mount photos, or pictures from behind the mirror and they show through these clear windows on the other side, actually creating a mirrored mat.

Once step #1 has been successfully accomplished and the mirror plating has been exposed, it is necessary to test Strip Silver part #2. Dab a small amount of part #2 onto the mirror plating. This reaction should immediately dissolve the mirror silvering. If not, the mirror manufacturer has applied an additional protective coating on the silvering which requires an additional application of Strip Silver part #1 before it is possible to proceed with Strip Silver part #2.

How much area of the mirrors **protective backing paint** should I remove? Answer: Remove an area slightly larger than overall stencil size. If you are working on a smaller project, remove the entire protective painted area.

Step 1: Cover your work area with several layers of newspaper. It is important to provide adequate ventilation during this process. Place mirror with painted side facing up towards you. Shake Strip Silver part #1 for one minute, then hold can approximately 8 to 10 inches from the painted surface and spray side to side in an overlapping pattern until entire area is covered with a generous layer. Wait 5 to 10 minutes. (See Photo S1) The painted surface will start to wrinkle, bubble and lift slightly off the mirror plating.

This is accomplished by a 2 step process...the first part or process removes the painted protective backing from the mirror. The second process allows you to remove selected areas of the mirror plating. After all a mirror is nothing more than a piece of glass that has been plated.

There are so many different types of painted mirror backings and silvering processes that it is necessary for you to test these mirror removing products to insure they will work with your particular mirror. Our Strip Silver Part 1 Remover works on about 80% of the mirror backings used. Some manufacturers use an epoxy based paint that is so tough our Strip Silver Remover is not strong enough to re-move it. Some use two or three coatings. Remember always test.

We recommend testing on a scrap piece of mirror, if this is not possible test these products on a small area at the edge of the mirror that is not visible when your project is framed. Follow step #1 to determine if Strip Silver part #1 will remove the protective paint backing. If no reaction is observed, repeat step #1 but this time after waiting 10 to 15 minutes, use a soft cloth to aid in the removal of the painted backing.

Step 2: Put on your gloves. Use a tissue to lift off the layer of painted backing and place it on the newspaper for disposal later. (See Photo S2) If some of the areas have not lifted, re-spray and

Photo S2

repeat step 1. When all the paint has been removed, very carefully clean the exposed silver surface with a soft cloth moistened with window cleaner.

Rub gently to avoid scratching the mirror plating but be sure to remove all traces of Strip Silver part #1.

Photo S3

Step 3: Completely cover the back of the mirror with contact adhesive vinyl. Determine the size and shape of the mirrored areas you want to strip out and draw or transfer them onto the adhesive vinyl. Use a hobby knife to cut out and remove these areas.(see Photo S3)

Step 4: Plastic gloves should be worn to avoid staining your hands. Brush on Strip Silver Part#2. Immediately upon contact the silvering will begin to dissolve. Use your brush to distribute part #2 over the entire cut out area until all the silvering is removed. This will only take a few minutes but time will vary according to the mirror itself and the size of the areas your stripping.

Step 5: Use a paper towel to blot up all the excess Strip Silver Part #2. Lightly moisten a

soft cloth with window cleaner and gently remove all remaining part #2. Use care not to scratch the plating. Remove the contact vinyl very slowly. Start at one corner and just lift a little area to determine whether the adhesive vinyl is pulling off the mirror plating. If it is use a hair dryer to lightly heat the adhesive vinyl making it easier to remove without harming the mirror plating. When all the adhesive vinyl has been removed, spray the entire back of the mirror with clear lacquer.

The lacquer will serve as a protective coating to prevent the mirror from oxidizing and turning black. Check out an old mirror...see those dark

Photo S4

spots that you can never wash off, well that's the mirror plating starting to oxidize.

You may choose to place photos or artwork behind the open areas, or you may paint them, place colored foil or paper behind the openings as accents. Combine etching on the front surface of the mirror combined with Strip Silver on the back of the mirror.